Cassius Chronicled

Jadon Lane

BookLeaf Publishing

Presentation by *BookLeaf Publishing*

Web: www.bookleafpub.com

E-mail: info@bookleafpub.com

ISBN: 9789357445023

First edition 2021

DEDICATION

Dedicated to my brother Mitchell,

We grow together my friend

ACKNOWLEDGEMENT

First and foremost I want to thank God, without our conversations and your blessings I wouldn't be who I am today. I want to thank my Mother for not only being the best parent I could've asked for but for being my first inspiration as a poet herself, your pen was the blueprint for my own. I want to thank my older sister Ymani, I've admired every step you took since we were younger and you've supported my every endeavor, you're one of my best friends and I'm grateful we creatively walk together. I want to thank my sister KB, an endless well of wisdom, constantly inspiring me to push myself further, you've made a tremendous contribution and I can't thank you enough. I want to thank Chloe, the fuse to my bomb and the muse to my poetry. You've been the light behind these poems for some time now and a huge part of the reason I'm so determined to keep going, I want to thank you from the deepest part of my heart. I want to thank my brother Amaziah, your wisdom, intelligence and knowledge of self shows in every aspect of you, whether it be your music or casual conversation I often find myself either referencing something I've learned from you in my writing or having your music playing to keep me in the right headspace, thank you Chachi. I want to thank my brother Jason, someone who's always had a burning ambition not to be deterred by anyone, you influence me to not only make sure my mind is fit but my body as well, thank you Jason.I want to thank Morgan and Iyeona, two ladies I am grateful to have met, thanking Morgan for every powerful presentation of poetry I've ever witnessed from her and Iyeona for helping organize the very first poetry slam at our school at which I'd do my first performance at. I want to thank both of them for being wonderful friends. I want to thank Devin, you have a mastery of words, my friend and your appreciation for the little things in life is unmatched by anyone. I have countless quotes from you jotted down in my notes and I constantly rewind moments in your music whenever I discover a new sound or find the meaning you've weaved within the lyrics, truly a magician. I want to thank Cley, your extensive knowledge on the things you care about truly influenced me to look below the surface into all the things that matter to me, as you would say "you're the tops, man" you know I had to show out for Money Mandos. I want to thank Marah and my Mandolino's family. All those guest check pads I forgot to take out my back pocket are finally paying off you guys. Thank you

Marah for putting up with my slacking when I was too busy writing to take care of a customer and thank my coworkers for picking up that slack for me. I love all of you guys. I want to thank Col. Howard, I wrote incog-negro in your classroom, you always knew how important poetry was to me and that means more than you know, thank you for all your support, sir. I want to thank Mama Stevens and Mr. Butts, you were both the highlights of my days when I'd see you. I appreciate all you've done for me and all you've seen in me, I love y'all. I want to thank my brothers from the Village Deangelo, Victor, and Kenny. I'll never forget the days we shared growing up, you're all a part of the foundation that my values are built apart, I'll always have a special place in my heart for you fellas.

Lastly, a thank you to everyone who I've been lucky enough to call a friend in these past few years. If I forgot to mention you I apologize but I don't value anyone any less. Love to you all!

PREFACE

I created the persona of Cassius Lovehall to embody certain traits that serve as the antithesis of my own personality, when Cassius was at an open mic you'd hear a different story than when Jadon would perform. As I continued to write from these two perspectives I realized how one would help me learn from another, for example in the poem "Cassius in a depressive state" I wrote the solution to my sadness before I fully acknowledged that I was doing it. Around the writing of that poem specifically I came up with the acronym that would help combat my anxieties head on

F - Feel in Control
D - Don't Overthink
L- Love unconditionally
N- Never lose sight of what matters and what you want

Writing from the shoes of a man who was supposed to be my opposite helped me grow as a person after a while the poems I wrote as Cassius and the ones I wrote as Jadon would become indistinguishable, Cassius had evolved into a fully rounded person and no longer a Caricature of things that I believed were the opposite of myself.

Deliver us from Evil

Deliver all of us from evil, not just the evil that they teach you
I'm talkin' about an evil that leaves people scorned
they teach you that evil is just red men with horns but to me Evil is deliberately going against words you've sworn
To me Evil is the misconduct behind fraternity dorms
To me Evil is critiquing upon someone's form spoken with malice
To me a few dollars donated to charity don't make things balanced
To me Evil is conquered in silence
To me Evil is more than the violence
To me Evil is everywhere from Church steeples to Phony people somehow I keep on loving you
Even to me the reason isn't apparent
Maybe don't need a reason
Maybe Love is inherent
I ask, is there any justice in forgiveness?
Is my dance just as groovy if it doesn't seem as rhythmic?
Can my words be spoken truly if they're always written cryptic?

My higher self speaks through me once this mental weight is lifted
My voice seems to question when I ask for Angel wings
I know peace of mind is with this wisdom clarity brings
A forgiveness for myself for all of my smaller things

Needles

The difference here is minimal
Like differences from ashes to dust
The difference is the light and you're not bright enough to trust
Point at a mirror if you must but the blame is still 1- to- 3
Acolytes of a wartime but your accents the only refugee
Careful who you bring to war your battle buddy's like a son to me
The sun it beams and my skin gets blacker than an effigy
Wasn't it like 2 months ago you were joking' about how darker folks were hard to see? I'm sorry, there I go living in the past you'll have to pardon me but for the time being can you refrain from using that language I don't have any extra black cards on me
The thought itself just startled me
Picture me in those ill-fitting patagonia shorts and I'm sockless in some Sperry's walking up to every dude that looked like me asking him to teach me how to dougie
Wouldn't that be frustrating?
Maybe not

Maybe my "gangsta heart" has gotten so black
it's starting to rot
like "I pull out this glock and bullets they drop
they love me, they love-me-not
I wave it around and y'all tuck tales like your
pockets got fables from Aesop and you're
thinking I'm mindless cause I'm saying I hate
cops but I just can't help myself like I'm part of
the four tops"
That's not my caricature, but I can't tell you what
you know
I used to know dudes that look like me that hate
to lay with ladies of the same color
They must be terrible at Uno
You know... Maybe Umar was right about
somethin'
'Cause I'm up at night and these numbers start
crunching
Why am I fiending for this...paperwork?
I'm hustling backwards
I'm going against the mission
I didn't read the dossier
Y'all still trying to take me to church so I know
you didn't listen to Hozier
then I hear a "hey"
they say "This stack has so many needles, we've
just gotta keep searching and hope that time
doesn't leave you, it's only a matter of time til
one of 'em deliver us from evil, right?"

Effervescent

The artist suffers ego death, he goes next
And his weapon? Smith and Wesson
Second guess ends in finale of the mortal vessel
Feelin special every new rotation, death ain't patient
Mundane mondays feel like vacation
Can't rely on someone's spaceship when you're skies have been colonized
You're hero's name italicized
whatever floated your boat made it capsize
Now you swim in a sea of lies if you see with eyes
My apple pies ain't American
My angels swear they seraphim
I'm scared of him and her 'cause he was hurt and she wears murderers on her shirt, which is worse?
I'm in a hearse and you're cursing at my pictures
I wish you well despite you're contradictions
Super rich kids have blurry vision, 20/20 seems like superstition
2017, the golden standard, jolly rancher syrup stuck inside my molars

Snow is colder when your blood runs hot, it's
hard to stop the motors of my mind and time
ain't been kind
It's the eye of the beholder that convinces me to
smolder 'cause wide smiles ain't cute
neither are dark eyes or the bags they carry
clean fist make me look scary
I'll never be that man again
I'll never be him
I'll never be that man again
That man ain't my friend
Won't feel that feelin' too familiar
Can't allow it to begin
That man don't really represent what's really
found within

I'm 20 feet tall

Sometimes I talk too much to cover up the bite marks on my tongue
Somethings seem perfect, I'm still pretty young
And this boy has been a gun, a loaded one, since Y2K
And I thank God every sunrise I'm still alive today
It took 4 months to learn somethings they stay the same
And some people scared to change or To see you do it
And they'll see to it that you'll never leave this barrel if they couldn't or they'll make you think you shouldn't
They've got the gall to make you feel small
I'm true to mine and in this state of mind I'm 20 feet tall
A sad case, I've got a baby face, I'm only grown below the waist and in most poems I leave a blank space tailored for the place I'm in
Just like an iPhone 6 I'll bend
But I'll try not to explode when I notice that this galaxy just might be the 7th
And all 20 feet of me still small compared to heaven

Bury me with these poems

Bury me with these poems I want to show the angels how Cassius flowed when my pulse was better
My angel feathers struggle to flap to better weather 'cause they're dyed black
My dye pack must've busted mid-flight so ends divine delight
Zoom in my line of sight and dress me superfly like a kite
Loosen my strings they feel too tight all of my might is temporary so my pride wears me
Pretend these things are not real scary I say "C'est la vie"
Save me from me before somebody beats you to it
All these lines tell a different story but these lines are not congruent
And I lied, I'm not a truant I just left before you noticed
If my face ever looks too calm just know that face is bogus

I say my cruel words in prose and my pretty ones in poems
they be soft guys inside but to you they cannot show them
Your progressive thoughts are passive
To you a man is nothing if you can't predict his actions
I've always been a blend of 2pac and "off the wall" Michael Jackson
This is what I'm askin'
Do you fight for the full array or really just a fraction?
I summarize my yesterdays
It's been a bummer missing summer so I write her and I say...

To claim the moon

To some the moon is cold
To me? She lights my sun on fire
To you she comes at night
To me? the 24 entire
She always calls before she comes
Over that is
Her shoulder is cold as the fridge
To know that Jehovah witnesses this all through the winter
That's the November and December
Then I binge her like a drug
Bend her like the end of a rug
The moon has a coat and it feels real snug
As my thighs rest upon her throne I question
Was she ever a fan of me or was this fantasy?
She planted seeds and now this moonchild is in infancy, infinitely me
Look mom the moon is following me as you sat in the back of your parents jeep grand cherokee
I said the same as her name appeared on IG

Dear Summer

Dear Summer,

I know you won't miss me, but the steam from
your streams make my twist get frizzy
I've been stuck in the house reality won't let me
out so this mentality popped out that made Nana
and Mama proud
Behind these 4 walls ain't nothin here but my
thoughts so there's four generations of myself
that I've fought
I've been torn between everything that I've been
taught and this persona that spent the last 4
months outlined in chalk
I used to yearn for summer suspended sunroofs
and hummers now I'm feeling the hunger I need
room and board for hunger
so dear Summer, It's you that I miss because
these snapchat memories have been used and
dismissed
I spent a year pursuing poems and passions now
it's off to a life I'd considered old fashion
Fantasies of friends and me as attendees with
our names written on seats
Those thoughts belittle me

Those thoughts are overused like middle C in
shimmy shimmy ya by ODB
Summer taught me that nothing is owed to me
I just hope Summers as nice to these kids as she
was to me 'cause right now me and summer are
on a break
For right now at least

Players of the show

The power of a mortal man moved by foreign hands
Feet buried in the soil of a stolen land
With cards in hand, what's the master plan cause
I can't hide you sinnerman
lied to by a bitter man, shifty as the sands and
Vile as can be but I seek an audience with that "he"
He who will not notice me 'cause he's not noticing issues deeper than the sea
Deeper than "You owe me" especially when things aren't changing
I am black as Bernie Mac, I am the warmth in a cold night, I am 20 with a Tupac spirit and you can hear it when my blood reaches higher degrees
I am not defined by societies higher powers that be
I've got stakes at the ready for the vampires in my TV screen
'Cause they've been scheming things, a real Kenan thing
I've seen things I imagined
I've entered the dragon

I've seen more than just a seat at the table so no I won't play at your show
Ain't no out when the upside ain't on your side, ain't no foresight, ain't no complacency, ain't no letting go
So are you playing at the show or for the show?

Space, Love and peace

You and I share the same ending
Space, Love and peace
Space is for the face that you make when I speak out of turn
What I learned was silence was a virtue and all these virtues come with vices
Even the bird that sings the nicest is annoying when you hear him long enough
So I trust that the scowl drawn across your face is illustrated with the purest of intentions and love is an invention, unique to each creator
I find the purest loves will cater to who you are later in life
Try as I might but I can't help but say my brightest things at night
If we link in the daytime you can speak your peace but I can't guarantee I'll share mine
I find my peace in writing these blurred lines
I mean peace! not a temporary cease fire between the folks in the middle east
I mean peace! not a symbol I throw up when I see cameras and there's a burning in my cheeks

I mean peace! not both of y'all knowing there's
an issue but you refuse to speak
I mean peace! And I thank God everyday that
I've found mine but like I said, you and I share
the same ending so just give yourself some time.

I'm not ashy, I'm divine

Sometimes when I'm really ashy, you know like
fresh out the shower, the shade of baby powder
I'll stretch out, emphasize every dry patch on my
skin
Inside of them are the shapes of clouds and just
like that my blemishes become symbols of
divinity
Golden halos above my head, Golden halos in a
box beside my bed
Same purpose, symbol of status and natural
blessings
Can't be purchased, they render traditional
currency worthless and it's not perfect
Which in itself an impossible feat, blasphemy
Same gifts given to you were taken from me
Take what you see as a sign yo look under the
surface in whatever you seek
I trust the little things to get missed
I trust the story in the coils of these two-strand
twist
I trust my fire to be hot
I trust my life to lead me out of writer's block

I trust the purpose in every battle that I've fought

Game Over Screen

Most of my fantasies include a game over screen
Usually on national TV so people can see what I mean
Some of my dreams aren't just fly cars, fancy houses and pretty women
Sometimes just my name getting raised over the table at thanksgiving
Now to be fair some of 'em have friends and fam higher up while I'm livin' but some of that comes with uncertainty and that gives me the shivers
Nana was a caregiver raised me to love people
World saw me as litter, you and I weren't seen as equal
Imagine me on hands and knees at someone else's steeple
Priest with feet on me as an example for his people
Now my conversations with the Most High are direct phone calls
My nose faced skyward when I watch the snowfall
Saints and sinners in vicinities facing off with obscenities
Unfortunately neither sides wearing name tags

Put your king in check

Take a look at everything around you
Everything you hold dear
Maybe even make a list, I understand how easy it is for things to get missed
But I can guarantee there's a black woman that you should thank near
It's so often that we only show appreciation to a woman when we think that they're attracted
Ignore our transgressions enacted and shift the blame to whatever the last did
How long that's lasted, but listen it seems that there's a central issue that we've been missing that lies within us unlearning our isms
Claiming we're all dancing to the same rhythm but cover our ears when we hear that we're out of step
How many have wept from a man who claimed to honor his queen
How many men have slept, drifted yonder and upon awakening seen his dream
It's in that realization that fuels my motivation

So often I feel the swords of a not so united states and turn to a black woman and say "I know you can relate"
She says to me with a laugh "King, you don't even know the half"
I'm sure that king was in quotations 'cause when we feel that companionship more often than not their spot is left vacant
Right now these are just words, rhyming reiterations of words you've already heard
Unfortunately that's where my power ends and your empowerment begins
School your friends, knowledge is meant to be lent
As far as the movement protesting these police cannot be the extent
As you can see we've come the distance you can see the blisters on the soles of our feet but until we right these wrongs our journey is so very far from complete

Killing in the name of the new me

The average will need a higher comprehension for this chapter 'Cause I'll be speaking in the tongue in the people coming after
The preachings of your pastor teachin' people of their new gods reachin' the youth with a moissanite grill on their canine tooth
They play their game on mute, the clicking of their buttons is morris code for "Absolute"
I see the blonde hairs in their roots, dye packs filled with King Krule's ooz
Now we bangin' heads with new rules
I'm killing in the name of the new me, I take the time to think so I can say things truly
Slow down, just think things through
Peep game, that game was never on mute the sounds was just played through bluetooth,
Damn! my thoughts we're 50% from you
Now my temperament is hot like a fever
lately all I do is think of how June was hotter than July

As if you read my mind you played me like a
chess piece now you've got me siding with red
or blue like solutions are so elementary
Speak for me! Speak for me! SPEAK FOR ME!
none of you do
Ultimately it'll be a collective destruction that I
choose

Metal Gear Rising

Scars on the back are the shame of a swordsmen
Shine from his skin a sign he came from where the lords been
Scarred shins from his past of closely following
Above his chin chapped lips
Behind them, a dry tongue
No song unsung, an iron lung so the smoke don't seep in, my melon leakin' secrets
Anxieties heat seekin'
My metal gears rising, I'm eyeing Raiden synthesizing with those spine things
asking how many scars has he left on the backsides of the bad guys and is he still a good guy or does that mean he's switched sides
Only then I realize, abandonment of the morals is a mortal sin
What's stoppin' me from the very same hypocrisy or takin' the moral high ground as an excuse to never pipe down
I learned that silence was a virtue and wisdom uses you as a vessel
Knowledge should be shared too
God Loves he who shares gleefully so my experience ain't meant for just me to see

Cassius in a depressive state

I woke up this morning
A blessing in itself
Pulled the Weldon Irvine record off of my shelf
And sang Morning Sunrise
I stare at every pore on my face as I brush my teeth then I shave
I clean up last nights mess, Sometimes that helps me forget that I'm depressed
I'm never sad the same way twice so the remedy is different today
I make coffee downstairs, mom greets me gleefully
Today my smile is heavy and she sees
She kisses my forehead, hoping her baby gets relief
It's the same outcome I seeked
With all this love around me how do I still feel lonely
I eat facing the sun hoping he has the answers to my questions
He doesn't speak a word nut he gives me some direction F.D.L.N

The hardest questions have the simplest solutions
"Happiness is yours if given to yourself, that smile is temporary if it's a gift from someone else. Give yourself the love you hand out as charity, an unconditional self love is salvation from disparity"

Ballroom dancing in traffic

Picture this
I'm completely on a bended knee
I mean this boyz turned to a man
And I'm pouring out my heart to this woman, at least the best that I can
Then suddenly I can't get the lines from the voices inside my head
They go radio silent, and Jadon goes silent
There she sat on that stairwell, her face geared to the left, my eyes locked with her ears, her lips pursed waiting on my next verse
And my lips? well they danced quietly like I don't quite know the words to your song
I'm so afraid to get it wrong 'cause I know that somewhere in your music there's paradise
The type to make me want to sacrifice the future futile fights and dance frankly by the ocean on these nights
I'm no slave to my pride, I'm not afraid to admit when you're right
So I raise from my knees to my feet
Your hands clasped in mine

Then we sway gracefully
You still looked kind of peeved but you humor me
Your crown rested beneath my chin then cheek to cheek
Ella and Louie, tenderly
Previously this type of humility was a sin to me
I'd turn my back times like these just to show off my strength
but my trapezius muscles are the easiest to see through and you'd tried to get that through my peasy but I kept hearing what the men above me had said
"Wear it all on your chest and if it kills you lil' homie then at least you tried your best"
But that's not fair to you
To suffer the aftermath of an old war of which you're not a refugee
Ready or not that beast had come for me and it was killing me softly
But you were my wake up call, my morning coffee
The fuse to my bomb and the muse to my poetry
Come as you are, you are to me the physical embodiment of Nirvana
And we'll walk in step in mindfulness if you should so do me that honor

Roses really smell like boo boo

I watched the woman born from the bud of a sunflower shrivel before my eyes
Like leaves in the fall but far quicker
I would've loved to say her fade was graceful but tasteful wasn't exactly in her vernacular
I'd once use words like spectacular to describe her but one thing I'm not is a liar
Though I suppose she left me inspired, whether it was right or wrong as I write these poems I see that left was the problem
It was me who was leaving, believing her deceiving ended with me
Lets just say her glitter was just that shiny and any tiny swerving off course led me to be left on read
I studied the words she said, they bled off my blue phone screen
I thought "It must be me" what the hell is wrong with me
Thus the constant Cassius workshopping
Sometimes I stop me from saying anything from a list of many things

What would my boys think? What would she think?
I guess I overthought like I tend to do
Even now I'm probably putting in more effort just thinking of you
Because of you, it'll probably be a while before I take "I love you" personal

My Big Brother rides on my shoulder

This isn't a poem nor a diary entry but the words within me remind me I'm not empty
I think about my best friend who's dead and how every word I ever said swirls in my head
The days I question my purpose I think about if he ever got nervous and is it only 'cause his book is closed that his story seems so perfect
I remember plans he had and wonder if he should be here instead
My birthday passed and this year I'm older than my big brother and because childhood is over I won't have another
I wonder if he blames me, sometimes I do, I should've spoken up even about the little things, I blame our friends for hearing some of the events and treating him like a king
I don't know if I'll ever be ever to read this and not feel that sting
You died when I was 18 and you were 19, Now I'm 20

Each day after you died moved so much quicker
I'll make sure each year I grow your senior, we'll
both get bigger

Under the Buddha Tree

The scene was serene, under the Buddha tree I swing from a tire
Living is easy from what I'm seeing, limited view I still aspire
Oak tree, evergreen, red eyes I blame on spring,
My chest begins to sting
Aaliyah sings from the speaker we have propped up on the beach chair
Natural shades homegirl is blinded by her bleached hair
I feel the breeze wind blows through holes in my streetwear
Homie departs with a dap, my friends all shake to show that we care
Doorbell rings, with food it brings, the pizzas pretty, after a spritz of Irish spring, we feast like fiends and hit the city
Street lights don't notice u, speed is a must, we might speed bike seems like somebody's clocking us

Tense tight, my eyes beam right somebody's watching us maybe through binoculars unless my oculars are Judas
Civilians mocking us, I swear intent is to pursue us
I hear everything around me through a megaphone filter
My dialogue is minimum, vibrations off-kilter
Hazy return to the mothership, Big brother don't see us
Smile and wave through the house I hope my mother don't see us
So begins the epilogue to a lost episode 'cause I guarantee in the A.M all these memories won't load
It's only in this mindset that I question where days go but I'm quickly distracted by a tickle in my throat

My fall leaves turned 20

The changing of the leaves are talking to me
Amerie sings she brings memories of simple things
but it's just one thing that's got me trippin'
Recent were the days of mismatch socks and class skippin'
So why is it that I fear my youth slippin'
See this black don't crack so I know my skin won't sag
And my ambition is hot so I know Cassius won't miss a bag
But there are times I already miss the things I currently have
And times I'm nostalgic about things I haven't seen yet, Times I get embarrassed about a smile I was proud of
Times you just don't get me the way a huge crowd does
I'm reminded too often that that tomorrows not promised so I'm grateful for every second

Like the days I spent face buried in
shrimp-flavored ramen
I talk alot, a fact that's easily noticeable, but only
when I feel like something needs to be said so
my post are few
I learned alot in 365 X 20 like when your skin is
sweet honeybees long to be close to you
I wake up every morning and feel purposeful, it's
great
There's no mountain I can't be on, I'm
surrounded by a pantheon, Hoodies and
Headphones Vol. 1 Track 9
I'm living in a dream age and I keep those I love
in a special part of my heart, I feel y'all beating
under my ribcage

Incog-Negro

Left with no choice
Commit a heinous cultural sin
Try my damndest to blend while denouncing my skin
Asked why I don't act like them
Pretending to grin like "them" ain't my friends
Again and again they ask "do you live in the hood?" "Am I doing this dance right?"
I smile and nod yes while they do the blockboy shoot and claiming it's from fortnite
How lacking was I in foresight?
You enunciate your words and they're claiming you talk white
My dialect is imitation? therefore assimilation was imminent so tell me what would you do in the situation
Maybe I'll make them think I'm one of them
I'll make them think I'm learning
I'll pretend I think the spread of communism is really concerning
When they ask me if I'm black I'll say "I'm actually 84% German"
Treat the kids who sag their pants and wear Du-rags like they're vermin
Just for a moment, bear my burden

Your contemporaries idolize the hood and blast rap music but call you a "Nigger" when your back is turned
But you're afraid of being that guy, you're afraid of bridges being burned
"We get it, you're black!" you didn't accept disrespect so now you're ostracized 'cause you epitomized the militant behavior that your peers lacked
So what would you do? become the voice of a silent people and try and be some kind of hero? or do you find somewhere to blend, pretend, become incog-negro

www.ingramcontent.com/pod-product-compliance
Lightning Source LLC
Chambersburg PA
CBHW051740130826
49812CB00033B/939
9789357445023